SELF-LOVE THE BEST GIFT TO ONESELF

(35 things you need to do to love yourself and live happily)

James B. Greer

Table of contents

Chapter 1: What is self-love?

There's a ton of talk nowadays about self-love. It sounds perfect, however, what does it mean? How would we love ourselves and what difference does it make?
Before an individual can rehearse it, first we really want to comprehend what it implies.

Self-love is a condition of appreciation for oneself that develops from activities that help our physical, mental, and otherworldly development.Self-love implies having high respect for your prosperity and satisfaction. Self-love implies dealing with your necessities and not forfeiting your prosperity to satisfy others. Self-love implies not making due short of what you merit.

Self-love can mean something else for every individual since we as a whole have a wide range of ways of dealing with ourselves. Sorting out what self-love resembles for you as an individual is a significant piece of your emotional wellness.

Self-love additionally implies tolerating yourself as you are right now for all that you are. It implies tolerating your feelings for what they are and putting your physical, profound, and mental prosperity first.

Self-love implies that you acknowledge yourself completely, indulge yourself with thoughtfulness and regard, and support your development and prosperity.

Self-love incorporates how you treat yourself as well as your viewpoints and sentiments about yourself. Thus, when you conceptualize self-love, you can attempt to envision how you would help yourself, how you would converse with yourself, and how you'd feel about yourself that reflects love and concern.

At the point when you love yourself, you have a generally positive perspective on yourself. This doesn't mean you have an inspirational perspective on yourself constantly. That sounds ridiculous! For instance, I can briefly feel annoyed, furious, or frustrated with myself despite everything I love about myself. Assuming this is befuddling, contemplate how this works in different connections. I can love my child even though I in some cases feel furious or frustrated with him.

Indeed, even amidst my annoyance and dissatisfaction, my love for him illuminates how I connect with him. It permits me to excuse him, think about his sentiments, address his issues, and settle on choices that will uphold his prosperity. Self-love is a lot of something very similar. And that implies, assuming you know how to love others, you know how to love yourself!

Chapter 2: Why do we need to love ourselves?

#1 **Self-love lessens pressure**

Self-care is a huge piece of self-love. At the point when you love yourself, you perceive indications of burnout and can do whatever it may take to decrease your pressure. Without self-love, you probably won't accept that you merit a break. The possibility of helping "me" may be extremely difficult to acknowledge. You are subsequently bound to endure an unpleasant time in any event, when it harms. Individuals with sound self-love are more able to set aside some margin to focus on themselves when they're worried.

#2 **Self-love can assist you with creating better propensities**

The information recommends that caring for yourself can assist you with settling on better wellbeing choices. In a Health Psychology meta-examination of 15 examinations, specialists found that when individuals acknowledged themselves without unforgiving judgment, they were more roused to roll out sure improvements in their day-to-day existence. One review showed this was the situation when individuals started to stop smoking. Different ways of behaving included eating better and working out. Self-empathy assisted individuals with shaping new, better propensities.

#3 **Self-love works on your profound strength**

During difficult situations, it's not difficult to slip into despair. Contingent upon the climate you're in, you may be managing individuals who fault you for your difficulties. You could fault yourself. Self-love helps counter bad, basic self-talk and put things in context. Regardless of whether your battles are a consequence of an error you made, self-love urges you to gain from the slip-up and push ahead. This forms your profound versatility and sets you up for future difficulties.

#4 **Self-love works on your connections**

There's a typical saying that states you can't love others until you love yourself. While this jest is a piece outrageous, cherishing yourself works on your associations with others. At the point when you love yourself, you won't feel as subject to others for your feeling of worth. This assists you with defining limits or on the other hand, if fundamental, cut off unfortunate friendships. Individuals who love themselves likewise will generally comprehend themselves better, which assists them with distinguishing the sorts of connections they need or don't need.

Self

#5 - **self-love makes you more useful**

Delaying is an efficient executioner. To get yourself inspired, you could turn to cruel strategies. Certain individuals use the dangers of self-discipline to attempt to get moving on an undertaking, yet research proposes that is not a powerful inspiration. Having empathy for yourself when you procrastinate is better. Utilize your "disappointment" as learning a valuable open door for what's in store. Rather than being hindered by self-analysis, you'll feel lighter and prepared to make changes to your way of behaving.

#6 Self-love can assist with overseeing nervousness and sorrow side effects

Research recommends that individuals with elevated degrees of self-sympathy have a lower risk of creating tension or discouragement. This doesn't imply that you're unequipped for adoring yourself assuming you're restless or discouraged. It suggests that parts of self-love (like self-care, self-empathy, and positive self-talk) can assist with overseeing side effects. Self-love can likewise assist with liberating you from the normal conviction that dysfunctional behavior is some way or another your shortcoming.

#7 Self-love can build your joy

Tolerating and cherishing yourself is connected to higher fulfillment with life, and in this manner, more bliss. At the point when you're continually breaking down your imperfections and condemning your decisions, having a cheerful outlook on anything is difficult. Self-love urges you to think about yourself like a dear companion. You can recognize that you're noticeably flawed, yet deserving of acknowledgement and backing.

#8 **Self-love supports your certainty**

It's truly challenging to feel certain assuming that you're centered around scrutinizing yourself. Individuals with negative self-talk frequently battle with low self-regard. An absence of certainty normally follows. If you have any desire to feel more sure, self-love is an effective method for practicing that muscle. Perceive your value and abilities, be merciful when you're disappointed with yourself, and you'll see your certainty building.

#9 **Self-love assists you with accomplishing your objectives**

Self-love instructs that your fantasies merit need. It isn't selfish to pursue what you need throughout everyday life. Individuals might attempt to tell you in any case, yet for however long you're not stomping all over others to arrive at your objectives, you ought to carry on with life in the manner that satisfies you. Self-love additionally gives the devices you want to accomplish your fantasies, like decreased pressure, close-to-home strength, expanded efficiency, and certainty.

#10 **Self-love motivates others**

The idea of self-love can be very challenging. You may be dealing with the conviction that says self-love approaches selfishness. The advantages of self-love we've given so far may not be very persuasive enough. Think about this: adoring yourself helps others. Like joy, self-love can be infectious. Assuming that you model what a sound connection with self resembles, it helps other people see the reason why that is significant. They'll start to rehearse more self-care and self-empathy. Everybody around you - and not simply you - benefits when you love yourself.

Chapter 3: How to Learn to Practice Self Love

Give yourself a break. Breathe deeply, give yourself a small hug, and begin learning how to love yourself.

1. Cast Out the Idea That You Have to Be Perfect(overcoming perfectionism)

Assuming that you're thinking about how to rehearse self-love, begin by dumping great; amazing all around — body, life, The thought of flawlessness is misleading, and when you see it via web-based entertainment, it regularly conceals significant psychological wellness issues.

Never hope to be impeccable. It's great to realize that no one tries to a romanticized norm of flawlessness; everybody has their particular characteristics and characters.
There's a contrast between being a successful person and being a stickler. The two sorts of individuals need to succeed. In any case, successful people are roused to give a valiant effort, while sticklers are persuaded by dread, deadened by the possibility of disappointment. Before we examine how to conquer hairsplitting, the following are a couple of significant things to be familiar with it:

Compulsiveness can extraordinarily decrease our self-regard, delight throughout everyday life, and feeling of harmony, as it can prompt gigantic pressure, anxiety toward judgment, or stresses of deficiency.

Attributes of compulsiveness are frequently connected to emotional well-being issues, similar to nervousness, OCD, and stress.

Individuals who are sticklers placed strain to fulfill out-of-reach guidelines on themselves. They are profoundly incredulous of themselves and beat themselves up over whatever doesn't fulfill their guidelines.

Sticklers likewise dread that if they don't go for flawlessness, they will turn out to be low-achievers and not arrive at their objectives.

At times fussbudget's dread of disappointment is frightening to the point that they linger because they would prefer not to accomplish something by any means on the off chance that it isn't possible impeccably.

We hurt others when we get involved with the legend of hairsplitting, by setting unreasonable assumptions for everyone around us.

Step-by-step instructions to Overcome Perfectionism

1-Become More Aware of Your Tendencies

The initial step to conquering hairsplitting is becoming mindful of your stickler considerations and inclinations. Get some margin to respite and focus on your thinking designs around hairsplitting. You could take a stab at getting these considerations on paper, to comprehend them better. When we know about how we permit hairsplitting to grab hold of our lives, we will be more ready to adjust our self-talk around this issue.

2-Focus on the Positives

Believing everything should be wonderful implies that we will generally focus on the negative pieces of our work or of ourselves. Notwithstanding, we should put forth a cognizant attempt to likewise perceive the upside. For all that you're not exactly happy with, challenge yourself to recognize three things that you do appreciate.

3-Allow Yourself to Make Mistakes

At the point when we permit ourselves to commit errors, we can see that it's not the apocalypse when we fall flat. Botches are open doors for us to learn, develop and improve. One method for rehearsing this is by taking up another leisure activity that you'll likely not be great at on the first attempt. Rather than attempting to be "awesome" at it, center rather around partaking in the movement and gradually improving those getting skills.

What you could find is that errors are important to get to where you need to be.

4-Set More Reasonable Goals

Sticklers will generally lay out the ridiculous objective, due to incomprehensible principles. One method for relinquishing compulsiveness is to lay out objectives that are more feasible and SMART. We will feel substantially less focused and more certain about our capacity to arrive at our objectives when they are sensible and testing in a sound manner.

Accommodating TED Talk on Perfectionism

5-Learn How to Receive Criticism

Individuals who are sticklers will quite often have low self-regard since they think about reactions literally. In any case, valuable analysis that can help us learn and develop is significant. Attempt to perceive that solid analysis can be useful and is ordinary since it can permit us to improve. Slip-ups or stumbles are entirely typical en route.

6-Lower the Pressure You Put on Yourself

Recall that the individual who pressures you the most is yourself. Be thoughtful to yourself and practice self-acknowledgment by settling for the easiest option you set for yourself. Assuming you are as yet roused and giving your all, you're doing fine and dandy. There is no such thing as "great," yet we can be pleased with giving a valiant effort.

7-Focus on Meaning Over Perfection

Attempt to move your attention on tracking down importance in what you do, as opposed to attempting to impeccably make it happen. On the off chance that something gives us pleasure and motivation, it doesn't make any difference on the off chance that it's not done impeccably. There is greater satisfaction to be had in tracking down importance en route.

8-Try Not to Procrastinate

Fussbudgets can be infamous slowpokes, giving themselves a reason to relax it they can't guarantee that they go about their responsibilities impeccably. This can be truly pointless and more distressing over the long haul. The hardest part is continuously beginning, yet in any event, making a harsh layout of our work quite a bit early is not all that great, but not terrible either than nothing. Recall that it's OK on the off chance that your work is flawed with the primary attempt or first draft, and give yourself the elegance to keep chipping away at the venture.

9-Cut Out Negative Influences

We must likewise screen how things like virtual entertainment, TV and motion pictures, books, or digital broadcasts can build up compulsiveness. We ought to be particularly careful about how online entertainment advances a story of "hustle culture" and hairsplitting in our work. Assuming you want to restrict these channels or erase them by and large, this can likewise assist us with moving away from compulsiveness.

10-Go to Therapy

Ultimately, treatment can assist with our nervousness around hairsplitting. Mental conduct treatment (CBT) specifically can help individuals battling hairsplitting reexamine their considerations. Treatment can likewise assist you with bettering figure out the more profound purpose for feeling the strain to be great. Assuming that you observe that you're battling, treatment might be a decent choice to give you significantly more devices to defeat compulsiveness.

2. Understand That Sometimes Societal Expectations Offer Unrealistic Standards

You are unique on this earth and cannot reasonably be compared to anyone else. You are the only one to whom you should compare yourself.

Theodore Roosevelt said, "Comparison is the thief of joy."

Even if you meet that unattainable standard, you will always be unsatisfied because you need more since it is in our human nature always to be insatiably curious. Avoid comparing yourself to that unattainable ideal; doing so will make you feel bad about yourself and depressed. Remember, the more we compare, the more we lose ourselves.

3. Live in the Moment, Just for a Moment Every Day

Stop your never-ending search for anything better for a time, and just look within. Recognize your origins and the wonder of the present. Realize how fortunate you are to be a living, breathing, and functioning human being.

According to Psychology Today, mindful people tend to have higher self-esteem, more empathetic, and are more secure.

4. Daily Gratitude(Noticing your progress and effort.)

Daily gratitude is the key to happiness and loving yourself.

Start a gratitude journal, an Instagram channel, a blog, or just take three minutes every day to think about all the things you have to be thankful for, such as your health, your life, your friends, your country, M&Ms, how long that old pan has lasted you, or how the person on the bus let you off first.

When we get comfortable, we get ungrateful. Change that, and show gratitude every day. According to Harvard Health, gratitude can make you feel more positive emotions and research has shown it can improve your overall wellbeing.

5. Embrace the Fact That You Can't Control Everything

The only things you can control are the ones you can change, including your reactions. Recognize that, like the weather, you do not influence other people, their decisions, or their actions.

Instead of attempting to control everything in life, focus on how you respond to it. Do the best you can and then put your hands up and say, “it is in the hands of the Gods now,” letting everything work itself out rather than attempting to control everyone and everything. Everything finally resolves itself.

6. Self-Care

Society has taught us that taking care of ourselves is selfish, and, God forbid, this is what we fear most. In response, we exert tremendous effort so that everyone knows our goodness.

The price of being "good" in the eyes of society is, however, your happiness. Stop attempting to be "good" and start looking after yourself. Self-love or Self-care = Happiness.

Start to take up these 30 Self-Care Habits for a Strong and Healthy Mind, Body, and Spirit. Self-care is one of the best ways to practice self-love.

7. Check In With Yourself Emotionally

We live so much of our day outside of ourselves. We engage in conversations with others at work, at home, and on social media. We read stories, news, and the opinions of others. We give our time and energy to help those close to us. Our mental space is almost always occupied. But how much of your day is spent in internal conversation?

Spending time with yourself can often feel like another task on our miles-long checklist, but it's an essential part of taking care of your emotional wellness and mental health. Just as you would exercise your physical body, "working out" your inner world will help keep you balanced among the stress of day-to-day life.

HOW TO CHECK IN WITH YOURSELF

You've probably heard the phrase "check in with yourself" many times before. But what does it mean? Checking in with yourself means carving out time each day to ask yourself how you're doing. In this space, you can sort out your emotions, assess your physical and emotional needs, and make an intentional plan on how to address these needs moving forward.

Here are three ways you can check in with yourself each day:

DEDICATED SELF-REFLECTION TIME

Choose a time of day when you're the least likely to be interrupted,

Find a seat, get a cup of coffee, and share your day's events. What mood are you in? Sense that emotion. The greatest course of action is to learn to feel your sentiments rather than bury them genuinely. It's essential to stay in touch with your feelings if you want to keep practicing self-love.

This includes negative thoughts. Do they exist? Do they prove useful? Are they decent?

Before you say something unfavorable, consider whether it will benefit you. Does having this thought in any way improve me? Or is it merely impolite, dismissive, and harsh?

Stopping internal agony is one of the most crucial steps to happiness because we frequently abuse our minds. Say supportive and encouraging things. Negative beliefs will always impede self-love

JOURNALING

If you express yourself best through the written word (looking at you, list-makers), grab your notebook and set aside a quick daily writing session. Even one minute is better than none.

MEDITATION

Mindfulness is all about becoming aware of your emotions and watching them pass with non-judgment. The meditation seat is an excellent place to work on the skill of checking in and letting go.

THE SCIENTIFIC BENEFITS OF CHECKING IN WITH YOURSELF

Checking in with yourself is a form of mindfulness, and mindfulness practices have been shown to have positive benefits for your psychological health. In this review of empirical studies on mindfulness, researchers concluded that mindfulness boosted feelings of well-being and self-compassion, reduced emotional reactivity and psychological symptoms (such as stress, anxiety, etc.), and improved behavioral regulation (the ability to stay calm and manage emotions). With so many benefits for your emotional health, mindfulness should be an essential tool in your wellness practice.

8. Tighten Your Circle

Your social circle affects your whole life. Look at the five individuals you spend time with since they make up who you are. Are they favorable? Loving? Supportive? Or are they unfavorable, impolite, and abusive? Do they also value themselves?

If someone is bringing you down, such as a negative friend, an insulting partner, or an overpowering, overly opinionated aunt, remember that you owe them nothing. They don't owe you any of your time. Ditch, avoid, and continue.

Nothing can dim the light that shines within us. But that doesn't mean people won't try. Today let's give some thought to the people in our lives and the effects each person has on our mood. Some people never fail to lift our spirits. Energy is contagious and when we see loved ones, we feel our spirits soar. Just the thought of certain people will bring a smile to our faces. But certain other people have the opposite effect. Seeing them tends to bring us down. They are a drag on our spirits and mood.

Take an inventory of your circle of friends. It might be time to tighten your circle. Looking back on our lives, we see that we outgrew certain people. We no longer had enough mutual interests, or maybe our dreams just took us in another direction. That's all right. We are not here to please others and they're not here to please us. But we'd be foolish to continue hanging with people or in places that drag our spirit down. Disconnect from negative people and watch how your life improves. You will feel better and achieve more once you shed the weight of negativity. Life is too short to stress over people who don't deserve to be part of your life. A positive life is a process. Part of that process is moving away from people who dull our shine. Are you surrounded by people who make you feel good? You don't have to be who anybody else wants you to be. You are free to be who you want. Move forward with your encouragers and ditch the toxic discouragers.

9. Eat Healthier

Your mental health is impacted by what you put into your body. If you eat something you think is terrible, you sit and feel ashamed of yourself, not only biologically.

Don’t be hard on yourself; life is too short to be miserable because you ate. Remove the eating restrictions, stop dieting, and eat like a normal person. Eat natural foods that you enjoy to practice self-love. Your body will appreciate it.

10. <u>Get Moving!</u>

Don't simply join a gym and never visit. Try out a new sport or physical activity, then discover one that you like that makes you laugh and is enjoyable for you. Do that then!

Zumba, spin, mermaid swimming, dancer… there are a virtually infinite number of different sports. Try them out and see how happy you become! There are many ways to keep fit, even if you are busy.

11. <u>Clear Up Your Environment</u>

Get rid of all the haters on social media. All those relatable memes about drunken underachievers. It simply makes sense to fill your head with positive information because you will live a positive life since you become what you think.

12. Be Unique

Take pride in your differences and learn to love them if you want to develop self-love. This is what distinguishes you. If you think about how can I love myself better, then try to be unique.

13. Let Go of Toxic Relationships

End all toxic relationships. Seriously. Nobody should be a part of your life if they make you feel anything less than fantastic. It may take some time to figure out which connections in your life are poisonous.

It's critical to consider the connections that make you feel good and recognize those that negatively influence your life.

The people that don't support you should not be in your life.

It is possible to get out of a toxic relationship and move forward to find a positive, supportive and healthy relationship. The following tips can help to break free from toxicity:

Self-care — finding time to care for yourself and to learn to care about yourself again is a critical step in healing and re-balancing your priorities.
Reconnect — rebuilding or reconnecting with friends and family who love and care about you helps to align your emotional healing with positive relationships with trusted people.
Therapy — therapy and counseling are instrumental in understanding the destructive relationship dynamics of a toxic partner. Therapy also helps to

establish self-assurance and self-esteem, which is necessary to prepare for a healthy relationship.

A toxic partner can make changes and rebuild the relationship. However, he or she must be willing to do the work to make these changes and to learn new ways to communicate and interact as a healthy, supportive partner.

14. Letting go of grudges or anger that holds you back

(Forgive Yourself)

Grudges are feelings of resentment that can be unhealthy to the individual carrying them.

Do you recall the one (or maybe a few) times you did something that left you feeling regrettable, humiliated, or ashamed? Time to let go of that. Although you can't change the things you've done in the past, you can influence what happens in the future.

Consider it a teaching moment, and believe in your capacity for change. Give yourself the same grace that you would extend to someone else if they were imperfect.
Some ways To let go of a grudge;

1. Acknowledge The Grudge
Figure out what it is that's causing you to hold on to the grudge. You have to know what the problem is to solve it. When you allow yourself to see the real issue you can then choose to move forward from there.

2. Communicate
Grudges begin to take root as issues go un-confronted which is why it's helpful to clarify your feelings on the situation.

Think about whether your feelings are something you want to work through internally, or whether you want to talk it out with the other person.

3.See Things From Their Perspective

To gain a better understanding of the other person's viewpoint, try to put yourself in their shoes. The more you understand the person you are holding a grudge against, the easier it will be to let go of that grudge. The longer we hold a grudge the more difficult it is to forgive and move on.

4. Accept The Situation

Rather than stew in the grudge, choose to accept it for what it is. You can choose to create your own healing, without waiting for an apology from the other party.

5. Don't Dwell

Once you decide to let go of your grudge, make sure you keep going and don't look back. Don't put too much thought into the situation or continue to discuss it with others. Dwelling a grudge will only make it harder for you to let go. If the issue is ever brought up again in conversation, just change the subject quickly and leave it in the past.

6. Stay Positive

Instead of holding on to resentment, use this as a valuable lesson that can help you walk away with a better understanding of yourself. For every negative situation, there is a positive.

7. Choose To Forgive

Choosing to forgive does not mean your choice to forget. It's just accepting that no one is perfect and acknowledging that people make mistakes. Forgiving is not the easiest thing to do, especially if you've gone through a lot of pain, but it's the only way to truly have peace.

15. Meditate

Take time out to calm your mind every day. Breathe in and out, purge your ideas from your head, and then simply be. Meditation is a way to be more intentional.

Be aware of your thoughts, feelings, and desires. Live a life that accurately reflects this. You can include self-reflection into your routine by engaging in mindfulness practices.

16. Remember Who You Are

You have endured a lot, yet you have overcome it, growing stronger with each experience. Please keep in mind who you are.

You should welcome adversity because it will make life more fascinating and help you go where you want. Experiencing feelings like self-doubt is natural, but don't let it overconsume your thoughts.

17. permit Yourself to Love Your Body

Your body is a gorgeous and fantastic tool for exploration. Your body wasn't made only to be aesthetically pleasing to the rest of the world. It's not an elaborate vase. It is a tool that enables you to accomplish all of your life's goals.

Climb, eat, go places, go to work, knit… as if it were your child, and take care of your body. With nothing but love and the knowledge that everything is ideal just the way it is. Loving yourself and falling head over heels with your appearance is what self-love is all about!

We are instructed that achieving the ideal body will make us happy. You are familiar with that kind; it is an unattainable beauty standard frequently airbrushed over.

No matter how much weight you lose, how many goods you purchase, or how much plastic surgery you have. A body cannot contain happiness because there is nowhere for it to reside.

Happiness results from accepting oneself. Realize that having a body is what you need to feel secure, successful, and like you can do anything you want.

You can do whatever you want regardless of how your body is shaped, so stop spending time attempting to follow a particular diet type and instead get Happiness. It is found within.

18. Try Minimalism

A minimalist person is someone who has a simple, uncluttered lifestyle. They don't believe in owning things for the sake of owning things — they only keep what is truly important to them. Minimalists are often very organized and efficient and find satisfaction in pursuing meaningful relationships and activities

True joy and love can only be found by enjoying your possessions and experiences, not material possessions.

You want someone to tell you at your passing how wonderful your life was and how you accomplished everything you set out to do! Not that you were a hoarder or had a large collection of things. Happiness is appreciating what you already have that can result in amazing discoveries like cooking a healthy meal from scratch.

Here's an inspiring read recommended for you: If Money Can't Buy Happiness, What Can?

19. List Positive Things About Yourself

Make a list of your best traits and accomplishments the next time you feel joyous and in control of the universe. While it might sound a little cheesy, it can be a great reminder when you are having a less-than-stellar day. Although it may be challenging initially, developing this habit can help you learn to accept yourself.

20. Don't Be Afraid to Be Creative

Use your imagination and whatever other means you choose to express yourself. Whatever catches your attention—painting, writing, sculpting, constructing, music—leave your inner critic at the door. There are no right ways to be creative.

Creativity can be beneficial to your health, according to Forbes.

21. Learn Continuously

Learn, read, and try new things. Figure out what works for you.

Try. Don't just read this. Think, "well, that's interesting," and leave. Choose one of them, then put it into practice. Happiness is a daily discipline, not a switch.

22. Stop Being Too Tough on Yourself

Some people are naturally hard on themselves. They might have low self-esteem or grow up in an environment where criticism came, and praise was heard rarely. Other times there are psychological issues that lead to a person being hard on themselves or a disorder that makes them lack confidence. Determining why you are hard on yourself can sometimes be found through self-exploration, and other times seeing a therapist to find out why may help you to find the root of your lack of self-assurance.

Not everything you think is true. We all have a critic who wants to keep us tiny and secure. The drawback is that it prevents us from living complete lives. One of the biggest things that might prevent someone from loving themselves is being hard on themselves.

We are usually much harder on ourselves than others. Sometimes you can be your own worst enemy.

You're going to experience failure from time to time. It's inevitable. But how will it affect you?

During stressful times, we can find ourselves falling into traps, such as negative self-talking--those damaging things we say to ourselves that get in the way of our success.

"There's no way this will work." "It's impossible." "I suck at this."

Stop being so hard on yourself!

You need to recognize when you're being hard on yourself so you can kill negative thinking.

How?

Are you comparing yourself to others? Are you hiding or repressing your anger? Are you trying to do everything alone without a support system?

Stop!

Below is an infographic with 12 simple and inspiring ideas on how to stop being hard on yourself.

Her 12 powerful tips:

Your mistakes are part of your learning. Learn to be resilient in the face of failure. Don't compare yourself to others because you aren't them. You're you, so accept yourself for who you are, faults and all.

There is no right way to do anything. Don't limit your thinking to a right or wrong way--there's no right way to do the wrong thing, and no wrong way to do something right!

Stand up for what you believe, even if it's unpopular. Make everyone understand your big, crazy ideas.

Learn from people who criticize you. Don't let criticism get you down; let it inspire you to work your ass off!

Accept your weaknesses as your "features". You aren't good at everything you do, but nobody else is, either!

Look at your past as an adventurous biography. Your past isn't your identity and doesn't dictate your entrepreneurial destiny.

Don't underestimate your talent until you apply it 100 times. Are you applying your natural talents?

Every single problem you have is not unique. Put your problems in perspective and solve them faster.

Intelligence is relative, self-esteem is not. Stay positive, take care of yourself, forget about being perfect, and always keep improving yourself.

Express your anger creatively. Feel your anger, express it, and learn from it.

Surround yourself with people who want you to succeed. Having people you can trust and rely on will make you happier and feel better about yourself.

23. Manage Stress

In today's society, stress and change often are thought of as the same thing. Stress is a physiological and psychological response to situations the body and mind find to be overwhelming. We often ask ourselves how we should manage stress. There are many ways people manage stress and reduce the overall stress of day-to-day activities. With the fast pace of work and home, being constantly inundated with technology, and still wanting to have time to connect with those around us, our lives can feel overwhelming and stressful at times.

Manage how you live with these five tips to feel less stressed:

1. Use guided meditation.
Guided meditation is a great way to distract yourself from the stress of day-to-day life. There are many guided meditations available on the internet that can help you find 5 minutes of centered relaxation.

2. Practice deep breathing.

Deep breathing is a great way to reduce the activation of your sympathetic nervous system, which controls the body's response to a perceived threat. Deep breaths are taken for a count of five seconds, hold for two seconds, and released to a count of five seconds, can help activate your parasympathetic nervous system, which helps reduce the overall stress and anxiety you may be experiencing.

3. Maintain physical exercise and good nutrition.

Physical exercise and nutrition are two important components of how you respond to stress. When your body is healthy, your mind can be healthy and vice versa. Physical exercise is proven to be a great stress reliever and also helps to improve your overall quality of life. Nutrition is important as stress can deplete certain vitamins, such as A, B complex, C, and E. Maintaining proper nutrition not only helps your body feel better but your mind as well, which allows you to better combat stress.

4. Manage social media time.
Spending time on social media sites can become stressful, not only by what we might see on them but also because the time you are spending on social media might be best spent enjoying visiting with friends, being outside enjoying the weather, or reading a great book.

5. Connect with others.
Humans are social beings. You need to have connections with people to feel supported. Finding a sense of community — whether at work, with a religious organization, or through shared activities, such as organized sports — is important

to your well-being. Enjoying a shared activity allows you to find support and foster relationships that can be supportive in difficult times.

24. Setting Time-Boundaries

If you think about "how to love yourself," then it starts by focusing on yourself. Set boundaries on how you'll spend your time. Steer clear of time-sucking activities that don't add meaning to your life.

Also, don't feel guilty for saying no. Saying no occasionally does not make you a bad person; rather, it makes you clever.

25. Step Outside of Your Comfort Zone

Taking a risk is one of the best ways to show yourself, love. The joy we experience when we realize we have accomplished something we didn't know we could do is fantastic.

26. Treat Others With Love and Respect

We feel better about ourselves when we treat people the way we want. Everyone may not always return the favor, but that is their issue, not yours.

27. Celebrate Milestones

No matter how big or small, acknowledge your victories. Be happy with your accomplishments and pat yourself on the back. This is a wonderful method to love and be pleased with oneself. Celebrating achievements in your life might help you stay motivated.

28. Follow Your Passion

Are you aware of that thing that both excites and terrifies you? Although you've convinced yourself it won't work, the thing you want to accomplish. Get moving on that!

Self-love is a dynamic concept. It can take a lifetime to perfect, but it requires continuous practice. Be nice to yourself and persevere through the challenging moments, especially if you're on the road to finding your passion.

These are some ways of finding your passion:

1. Remember What You Loved as a Child

Often, our truest passions emerge in childhood, only to be squelched by real-life pressures. So think about what you loved long before you had to worry about your career. Writing? Science experiments? Taking care of people? Getting back in touch with those instincts is an important step in finding your passion.

2. Eliminate Money from the Equation

If money were no object, what would you do? Would you travel? Spend all of your time with your children. Would you start a charitable organization to help abused women? Of course, money can't be ignored, but don't let financial pressures dictate your choices. Your career should ultimately lead to financial security, but if financial security is the defining motivator, it's unlikely you'll end up doing what you love.

3. Ask Your Friends for Feedback

Sometimes you're just not the best judge of what makes you happy. Ask the people who know you intimately when you seem the happiest and what you do the most enthusiastically. Their answers may surprise you.

4. Read through a University Course Catalog

Find some quiet time and see which courses naturally interest you. What would you study if you could do it all over? What courses do you think you could teach? Which subjects scare you to death, and which ones do you find boring? Revisiting these possibilities will help point you in the direction of subjects and topics that you love.

5. Identify your Professional Hero

Of everyone you know, either personally or in your extended frame of reference (from your dermatologist to Oprah), whose career would you most want to emulate? Reach out to her to learn more about how she got to where she is, or, if that's not possible, read everything you can about her career and life.

6. Think of What You Enjoy That You Also Do Well

After you've done these exercises, think about what you've learned. Focus on the things that you both enjoy and do well—whether you have a way with animals, make a killer lemon tart, or are crazy for origami—and write them down. Then, narrow the list to the top three or four things. Keep it handy, review it often, and use it as your jumping-off point when you're plotting your career move.

29. Give up the Need for Approval From Others.

It's totally fine to look for others' approval on occasion. But there comes a point where it becomes a habit — which is when it's important to take a step back and recognize that you do not need someone else's approval to feel good about yourself.

Essentially, confidence and validation go hand in hand. "A lack of confidence stems from a lack of trust in ourselves," confidence coach Lisa Philyaw tells Bustle. "When we don't trust ourselves, then we look to others for approval. We trust their opinion more than our own, so we see their opinion as more valid because we're not trusting ourselves or our perspective."

"You can be the ripest, juiciest peach in the world, and there's still going to be somebody who hates peaches." — Dita Von Teese.

You don't need to rely on approval from others to love yourself. Giving up your need for approval from others will help you find your happy place and also help you let go of past trauma and wounds. Sometimes our want for approval is attached to events from the past.

The reality is that when we let go of the things that have happened to us, it feels almost as though a burden has been lifted. We are no longer required to transport that. We deserve better.

30. Find Your Happy Place

What is the one area where you feel completely at ease, at peace, happy, optimistic, and full of life? When going through a difficult period, visit that location or visualize yourself there. Consider the way something looks, feels, and smells. Make it a habit to regularly envision your happy location.

Research shows that happier people are more successful people. That's reason enough to make a point of being happy at work. But wait--there's more! Happy people have more successful relationships, better mental health, and live longer lives. Not bad for an emotion that you have control over.

Everyone should have a place where you can go to feel safe and happy," "It may be a place you can physically visit or, at times, even just imagine, but it must be a respite that recharges you."

Here are some tips on how to find that special happy place in the world:

1. RECALL PLACES WHERE YOU'VE APPRECIATED THE SOUNDS
Birds chirping, a brook babbling, beautiful music, people's voices.

2. SUMMON UP THE PLACES WHERE YOU'VE ENJOYED VISUAL IMAGES
An open view of the sky or sea, pleasing colors, and shapes, inspiring art or architecture.

3. CHOOSE A PLACE WHERE YOU CAN EXPERIENCE THE ELEMENTS THAT CONTRIBUTE TO HAPPINESS
Exercise, social contact with happy people, creative flow, laughter. Your

happy place, says Nancy, may also be a "low-stimulation environment with little of the above. Quiet stillness can offer a feeling of being at peace that can last for a long time."

4. REMEMBER WHERE YOU WERE WHEN YOU EXPERIENCED DEEP CONTENTMENT AND MEANING

It could be the playground where you took your children when they were young; the animal shelter or food pantry where you volunteer; or the café where you met your future spouse.

5. STAY OPEN-MINDED

Studies in the Journal of Environmental Psychology show that spending just 20 minutes in nature boosts vitality levels significantly. Others may prefer a favorite spa, an indoor Zen retreat with candles and soothing music, or a kitchenware store filled with gleaming pots and exotic ingredients.

31. Turn Off and Inwards

Grab a cup of your preferred tea, coffee, wine, or other beverage, and sit by yourself for a while. Just you, no TV or other distractions. Consider the amazing things now taking place in your life, your greatest aspirations, and the best ways to achieve them.

32. Try Journaling

Journaling is an incredibly beneficial self-care technique, which doesn't just enhance feelings of happiness, but reduces stress, clarifies thoughts and feelings, and ultimately helps you get to know yourself better.

How do you feel your head is spinning so much from having so many thoughts? No matter how bizarre, cruel, depressing, or horrifying they are, list them all on paper.

Whatever it takes for you to let it go, do it. Keep it in a notebook. Regular journaling can be a crucial component of your self-love practice and will help you gradually recognize the value.

33. Be Realistic

Being realistic means becoming aware of your own biases, flaws, and internal assumptions. Having a clear-eyed view of yourself can help you decide which traits and beliefs are helping you and which ones you need to change.[11] However, make sure that you do not compare yourself to other people. Just stay focused on yourself.

Nobody on this planet experiences happiness every second of every day. Do you understand the reason? We are all human, after all. We all make errors and have mixed emotions, and that's okay. Embrace your humanity.

You can develop a realistic mentality by practicing it. We are often overly hard on ourselves, so learning to be realistic will aid you in your quest for self-love.

34. Laugh

There are many benefits to laughter, and it's a part of self-care. Learn to do things that make you laugh and spend your day joyously.

It's true: laughter is strong medicine. It draws people together in ways that trigger healthy physical and emotional changes in the body. Laughter strengthens your immune system, boosts mood, diminishes pain, and protects you from the damaging effects of stress. Nothing works faster or more dependably to bring your mind and body back into balance than a good laugh. Humor lightens your burdens, inspires hope, connects you to others, and keeps you grounded, focused, and alert. It also helps you release anger and forgive sooner.

With so much power to heal and renew, the ability to laugh easily and frequently is a tremendous resource for surmounting problems, enhancing your relationships, and supporting both physical and emotional health. Best of all, this priceless medicine is fun, free, and easy to use.

As children, we used to laugh hundreds of times a day, but as adults, life tends to be more serious and laughter more infrequent. But by seeking out more opportunities for humor and laughter, you can improve your emotional health, strengthen your relationships, find greater happiness—and even add years to your life.

Laughter is good for your health

Laughter relaxes the whole body. A good, hearty laugh relieves physical tension and stress, leaving your muscles relaxed for up to 45 minutes after.

Laughter boosts the immune system. Laughter decreases stress hormones and increases immune cells and infection-fighting antibodies, thus improving your disease resistance.

Laughter triggers the release of endorphins, the body's natural feel-good chemicals. Endorphins promote an overall sense of well-being and can even temporarily relieve pain.

Laughter protects the heart. Laughter improves the function of blood vessels and increases blood flow, which can help protect you against a heart attack and other cardiovascular problems.

Laughter burns calories. Okay, so it's no replacement for going to the gym, but one study found that laughing for 10 to 15 minutes a day can burn approximately 40 calories—which could be enough to lose three or four pounds for a year.

Laughter lightens anger's heavy load. Nothing diffuses anger and conflict faster than a shared laugh. Looking at the funny side can put problems into perspective and enable you to move on from confrontations without holding onto bitterness or resentment.

Laughter may even help you to live longer. A study in Norway found that people with a strong sense of humor outlived those who don't laugh as much. The difference was particularly notable for those battling cancer.

35. Recognizing your strengths
What are your Strengths?

Strengths are a unique combination of your skills, talents, knowledge, and experience. You have many Strengths, some are obvious, but many others aren't. Many of your Strengths go underutilized, unappreciated, and too often, unrewarded. Is it easier for you to name your strengths or your weaknesses?

Many of us are keenly aware of our weaknesses, but struggle to identify our natural strengths and talents.

Even more, when prompted to think of something we want to improve about ourselves, many of us likely think of a weakness. Not a strength.

But research shows that people who recognize and regularly use their strengths are more successful at work. When we focus on developing our strengths rather than trying to improve our weaknesses, we experience faster growth.

Chapter 4:Final Thoughts

You can improve your relationship by learning to love yourself and practicing self-love. This is essential if you want to develop a strong connection with other people. Although it takes time to develop self-love, you will undoubtedly get better at it.

Even if you're under stress, consider all that you've already accomplished. You will be one step closer to being the best version once you discover how to be kind to yourself.

A wonderful time! Get out there and pursue the activities that ignite your passion. Enjoy them, enjoy who you are, and take in your amazing life.

www.ingramcontent.com/pod-product-compliance
Lightning Source LLC
LaVergne TN
LVHW052054160826
845678LV00015B/3228

* 9 7 9 8 8 4 4 2 3 3 3 0 2 *